RETREAT GUIDE

CHRIST ALONE
IS ENOUGH

A RETREAT GUIDE
ON ST. PAUL'S LETTER
TO THE COLOSSIANS

FR. JOHN BARTUNEK, LC, STHD

This booklet is a part of RCSpirituality's *Retreat Guide* service, which includes free online videos and audio tracks available at **RCSpirituality.org**.

INTRODUCTION

Christ Alone Is Enough

RETREAT OVERVIEW

Every year during the Christmas season, the Church's liturgy brings our attention to St. Paul's Letter to the Christians who lived in Colossae, a city in the Lycus River valley, in modern day Turkey. St Paul wrote his letter from prison, probably in Rome. He had heard that the young Christian community in Colossae was experiencing turbulence. Some teachers there were claiming that Jesus, and the grace Jesus gives, were not sufficient for our salvation. Instead, so these teachers affirmed, we need to add on the mediation of angels and other spiritual forces, as well as various ritual practices that worked almost like magic when combined with special, secret knowledge beyond what Jesus had taught.

St. Paul recognized the danger in these kinds of false doctrines. His Letter to the Colossians functions as a kind of inoculation against them, and against the deadly virus of spiritual self-sufficiency that they were spreading. And that's a virus that has reappeared in our own age, morphing from its pre-Christian form into a post-Christian, secular form, but still as dangerous as ever.

In this Retreat Guide on St. Paul's Letter to the Colossians, we will have a chance to renew our inoculation. We won't be able to go through the whole Letter. We will focus on some important highlights that, hopefully, will enable you to read the whole Letter on your own and get more out of it than ever before:

o   In the two Meditations, we will touch on crucial passages linked to authentic, Christ-centered spiritual freedom.

o And in the Conference, we will review the ancient practice of *Lectio Divina*, sacred reading, as a way to follow St. Paul's advice to the Colossians to "let the word of Christ dwell in your richly." The Conference will reflect on the symbolism present in the image itself, symbolism that can help stir up the spirit of Christmas in our souls.

Let's begin by quieting our hearts and turning our attention to the Lord, who never stops paying attention to us. And let's ask him for all the graces we need, most especially, the grace to discover, once again, that Christ alone truly is enough.

NOTES

FIRST MEDITATION
The Danger of Spiritual Worldliness

INTRODUCTION

In Chapters 1 and 2 of his Letter to the Colossians, St. Paul extends a warm and affectionate greeting, and then gets right into the substance of his concern by asserting the preeminence and sufficiency of Christ, warning readers against any kind of teaching that would detract from that. In this context, St. Paul writes: "See to it that no one captivate you with an empty, seductive philosophy according to human tradition" (Colossians 2:8).

This is the real heart of the matter, and it touches on something relevant not only two thousand years ago for the Colossians, but for Christians of every time and place: the temptation to spiritual self-sufficiency.

A MISTAKEN IDEA OF HOLINESS

As fallen human beings, we would like to figure everything out once and for all. We would love to find the perfect formula to solve all our problems. We are always tempted to think we can create heaven on earth, uncovering the definitive secret to absolute happiness. We even sometimes think that holiness—the fruit of healthy Christian living—will somehow free us from all ills, sufferings, and confusion; but that is a mistaken idea of holiness.

The truth is that, as long as we are still living here on earth, we will never figure everything out or solve all our problems or find the one secret to perfect happiness. Our earthly lives are a journey to our heavenly home, a pilgrimage of faith that only ends with death. And throughout this journey, we will always find new mysteries to explore, new challenges to meet, new obstacles to overcome. That's the nature of a pilgrimage. If we have Christ, we have all we need for a successful journey. And if we travel with him faithfully, our lives will take on more and more meaning and exhibit more and more fruitfulness for his Church, but we always have to keep on traveling. Any doctrine that promises an end to the journey on this side of eternity may be, as St. Paul says, "seductive", but it is also "empty," and it is certainly nothing more than "human tradition."

THE PERENNIAL TEMPTATION

The temptation to find perfect happiness in some sort of secret knowledge or special ritualistic behavior is as old as humanity itself.

Do you remember how the devil tempted Adam and Even in the Garden of Eden? He made them doubt the wisdom of God's command, and then he gave them a false promise about what would happen if they ate the forbidden fruit: "…[W]hen you eat of it your eyes will be opened and you will be like gods" (Genesis 3:5). To be like gods, to be divine, independent, self-sufficient, eliminating the discomfort of mystery and trading in life's pilgrimage for a false but comfortable "enlightenment"—this was the original temptation, it was at the root of the disturbing doctrines in Colossae, and it is still with us today. Here's how the Catechism describes it:

In that sin man preferred himself to God and by that very act scorned him. He chose himself over and against God, against the requirements of his creaturely status and therefore against his own good. Constituted in a state of holiness, man was destined to be fully "divinized" by God in glory. Seduced by the devil, he wanted to "be like God", but without God, before God, and not in accordance with God.

—CCC 398

MODERN VERSIONS OF ANCIENT HERESIES

Pope Francis refers to contemporary forms of this spiritual self-sufficiency as modern Gnosticism and Pelagianism. These are ancient heresies with long and complex histories. But for Pope Francis, their manifestations in our post-Christian, secular world are easy to spot. He describes them as a kind of "spiritual worldliness" that "hides behind the appearance of piety and even love for the Church" but ultimately "consists in seeking not the Lord's glory but human glory and personal well-being." Here's how this "spiritual worldliness" expresses itself, according to Pope Francis:

This worldliness can be fueled in two deeply interrelated ways. One is the attraction of gnosticism, a purely subjective faith whose only interest is a certain experience or a set of ideas and bits of information which are meant to console and enlighten, but which ultimately keep one imprisoned in his or her own thoughts and feelings. The other is the self-absorbed promethean neopelagianism of those who ultimately trust only in their own powers and feel superior to others because they observe certain rules or remain intransigently faithful to a particular Catholic style from the past...

—*Evangelii Gaudium*, 94

These are the exact kind of patterns St. Paul warns against throughout his Letter to the Colossians.

Whenever we take our eyes off Jesus, looking instead to formulas or check-lists or devotions that appear to promise holiness as an automatic result of connecting certain intellectual or behavioral dots, we are exchanging Christ's saving grace for comfortable self-help techniques. This kind of spiritual worldliness (often subtly encouraged by our spiritual enemies) can only distance us from God's grace and weaken our friendship with Christ. That is what St. Paul meant when he wrote:

❝See to it that no one captivate you with an empty, seductive philosophy according to human tradition, according to the elemental powers of the world and not according to Christ.

—Colossians 2:8

SEEKING WHAT IS ABOVE

But what's the antidote? In St. Paul's words, it's very simple. He starts out Chapter 3 of this Letter making it as clear as possible. He writes:

❝If then you were raised with Christ, seek what is above, where Christ is seated at the right hand of God. Think of what is above, not of what is on earth. For you have died, and your life is hidden with Christ in God. When Christ your life appears, then you too will appear with him in glory.

—Colossians 3:1–3

We have indeed been raised with Christ, because we died with him and were buried with him—that's what happened, sacramentally speaking, when we were baptized. So now our very souls have been touched with grace, so that the same life that is Christ's life animates us from within: "you have died, and your life is hidden with Christ in God…Christ your life…"

This is an objective reality. It happened. It was God's gift. So now our task, our great adventure, is gradually to let this new life within us grow and unfold. And God has chosen to let us be partners in that unfolding.

This is why St. Paul encourages us to "seek what is above" and to "think of what is above." In contrast to spiritual worldliness, which tries to find ultimate fulfillment once-and-for-all in earthly terms, we as Christians are called to continue deepening our personal knowledge of Jesus as we daily renew our providentially guided journey home. Believing in Jesus is not a self-help technique to be mastered as a fix for all our ills. Believing in Jesus is truly a relationship of love that invites us, day after day, to freely and wisely decide to "seek what is above, to think of what is above," that is, to discover afresh each day how to live our lives as Jesus would have us. That is our ongoing task, and that is what will gradually fill our hearts and minds with the fruits of the Holy Spirit.

A LESSON FROM THE LITURGY

The Church's liturgy places those precise words of St. Paul in the Second Reading for Mass every Easter Sunday. It's a powerful reminder of the preeminence and sufficiency of Christ, and of our joyful privilege to be his brothers and sisters, and to choose always and everywhere to be his followers.

In the next meditation we will examine St. Paul's description of what life in Christ looks like in practical terms. But for now, let's take some time, in the quiet of our hearts, to reflect prayerfully on the difference between a Christ-centered spirituality and spiritual worldliness. The following questions and quotations may help your meditation.

QUESTIONS FOR PERSONAL REFLECTION/GROUP DISCUSSION

1. What worldly influences around me tend to make me think that I can have heaven on earth? How do I tend to respond to those influences?

2. Is my personal friendship with Christ still growing? What has helped it grow in the past? What is helping it grow now? What is hindering its growth?

3. What do I do on a daily basis to choose to "seek what is above" and "think of what is above"? How could I do that more intentionally?

QUOTATIONS TO HELP YOUR PRAYER

❝Though holy doctors have uncovered many mysteries and wonders, and devout souls have understood them in this earthly condition of ours, yet the greater part still remains to be unfolded by them, and even to be understood by them. We must then dig deeply in Christ. He is like a rich mine with many pockets containing treasures: however deep we dig we will never find their end or their limit. Indeed, in every pocket new seams of fresh riches are discovered on all sides.

—St. John of the Cross
EXCERPT FROM *A SPIRITUAL CANTICLE*,
OFFICE OF READINGS FOR DECEMBER 14TH

❝If then you were raised with Christ, seek what is above, where Christ is seated at the right hand of God. Think of what is above, not of what is on earth. For you have died, and your life is hidden with Christ in God. When Christ your life appears, then you too will appear with him in glory.

—Colossians 3:1–3
NABRE

❝This worldliness can be fueled in two deeply interrelated ways. One is the attraction of gnosticism, a purely subjective faith whose only interest is a certain experience or a set of ideas and bits of information which are meant to console and enlighten, but which ultimately keep one imprisoned in his or her own thoughts and feelings. The other is the self-absorbed promethean neopelagianism of those who ultimately trust only in their own powers and feel superior to others because they observe certain rules or remain intransigently faithful to a particular Catholic style from the past...

—*Evangelii Gaudium*, 94
POPE FRANCIS

NOTES

SECOND MEDITATION

Walking in Christ

INTRODUCTION

In the first meditation, we saw how St. Paul warned the Colossians against spiritual worldliness, against thinking that special knowledge or rituals could take the place of life in and with Christ, the only source of authentic hope and true spiritual progress. He summarized the authentic, Christ-centered approach to spiritual growth like this:

❝So, as you received Christ Jesus the Lord, walk in him, rooted in him and built upon him and established in the faith as you were taught, abounding in thanksgiving.

—Colossians 2:6–7

We have *received* Christ, through baptism, through faith, through our years of prayer and receiving the other sacraments. And now St. Paul exhorts us to "walk in him" and to stay "rooted in him and built upon him." In other words, Christ alone is enough, and the more he becomes the center and the source of all our living, the more our faith will flourish and the more we will experience the meaning, purpose, and joy of the saints.

A RELIGIOUS SURPRISE

And what does a Christ-centered life look like in the concrete reality of daily life? St. Paul gives us a portrait of it in Chapter 3. It would have been a surprising portrait for many of the Christians in Colossae. At the time, religion in the ancient world was obsessed with complex rituals and esoteric practices. The more religious a person was, so it seemed to both the pagans and the Jews at the time, the more removed that person was from the ordinary activities and concerns of life of earth.

But for St. Paul, faith in Christ leads not *away* from ordinary life, but more deeply *into* ordinary life. Faith in Christ gradually releases our full human potential, so that holiness blossoms not primarily in weird, elitist ceremonies and customs, but in simple virtue. "Walking in Christ," therefore, means first and foremost living as Christ lived, freely choosing to do and say what is right and good in every situation, whether it's convenient or not. That is how we exercise our God-given freedom in such a way that our spirits flourish and life becomes truly meaningful.

PUTTING AWAY THE OLD SELF

St. Paul describes Christian living first of all by identifying the self-centered behavior patterns—vices—that lead to spiritual frustration. This is the way of life of the pagan who has not experienced God's love and forgiveness. But even Christian believers can fall back into a pagan lifestyle, because "walking in Christ" requires us to choose Christ daily—we can't just switch on some kind of spiritual autopilot and expect authentic growth in holiness. God has chosen to make us partners in our own salvation, so we have a real role to play in following the Lord.

Here is St. Paul's exhortation to leave behind the old, self-centered way of life that contradicts our new life in Christ:

Put to death, then, the parts of you that are earthly: immorality, impurity, passion, evil desire, and the greed that is idolatry. Because of these the wrath of God is coming [upon the disobedient]. By these you too once conducted yourselves, when you lived in that way. But now you must put them all away: anger, fury, malice, slander, and obscene language out of your mouths.

—Colossians 3:5–9

30

Notice how much confidence St. Paul has in our capacity to resist temptation. He encourages us to "put to death" these worldly tendencies, to "put them all away." This implies that we are not completely at their mercy. And this is true. In Christ we have received God's grace, which gives us light to know and strength to choose what is good and right. God's grace is at work in us, but it's up to us to cooperate with that grace. Here we find an expression of our dignity as Christians. As St. Augustine put it a few centuries after St. Paul: "God created us without us: but he did not will to save us without us."[1]

PUTTING ON THE NEW SELF

But Christianity isn't just a list of sins and vices to avoid. We only resist those kinds of temptations so that we can embrace what St. Paul elsewhere calls the "glorious freedom of the children of God" (Romans 8:21). This freedom is the flourishing of our human nature in general and the healthy development of each person's unique gifts. That is how we glorify God and experience life as God meant it to be.

The path to this flourishing and development is what Christian tradition refers to as the virtuous life. Here is how St. Paul summarizes it in his Letter to the Colossians:

Put on then, as God's chosen ones, holy and beloved, heartfelt compassion, kindness, humility, gentleness, and patience, bearing with one another and forgiving one another, if one has a grievance against another; as the Lord has forgiven you, so must you also do. And over all these put on love, that is, the bond of perfection.

—Colossians 3:12–15

1   Quoted in the *Catechism of the Catholic Church*, #1847

St. Paul chose his words carefully, and he was writing under the Holy Spirit's inspiration. So let's go through this passage phrase by phrase, savoring this portrait of our own Christian identity.

NOT A PERFORMANCE-BASED SPIRITUALITY

As St. Paul encourages us to "put on" these virtues, to choose to live and act in this way, he reminds us of the *why* behind the what. He reminds us that we are "God's chosen ones, holy and beloved." This is critical.

Christian life is not about earning God's love by performing virtuously. It isn't about what we can do for Christ or what we can do to make ourselves holy and acceptable to God. That's a backwards view of the whole Christian endeavor. Christian living doesn't start with our efforts; it starts with God's grace. It starts with God choosing us, out of love, while we are still broken and alienated because of original sin and personal sins. His loving choice overflows in the gift of his grace, which renews us from within and makes us his children, sharers in his own nature—what Paul calls in this passage, "holy".

St. Paul starts there. Only when we realize that we are chosen, beloved, and graced by God are we truly ready to cooperate in the unfolding of that grace through "putting on" the list of virtues that follow.

CHRIST-LIKE LIVING

And what are the different virtues that make up the Christian's spiritual wardrobe? The first five St. Paul mentions all have to do with how we treat other people.

This is significant. We are created in the image of God, and God is a Trinity—three persons, one divine nature. So the grace of God that renews our hearts will renew us in how we relate to other people. Having discovered that we ourselves are valued and prized by God, that we are his "chosen ones, holy and beloved," we also discover the freedom to treat other people as God has treated us. This is how God's grace redeems the fallen, divided world. And so the virtues that the Christian lives begin with how we relate to each other.

o   St Paul starts his list with "heartfelt compassion." This is our internal attitude towards our neighbor, the attitude that seeks to understand and accept, not to judge and condemn.

o   He then moves on to "kindness," the external expression in word and deed flowing from internal attitude. Kindness actively builds up our neighbor, avoiding damage and hurt.

o   Humility keeps us from forcing our own will on other people, or arrogantly undervaluing them. Humility reminds us that only God is God, and each one of us is wholly dependent on him and loved by him.

o   Gentleness and patience come next. Gentleness guards us from the two extremes of anger and indifference, while patience leads us never to give up on our neighbor.

o   He finishes his list with forgiveness, the virtue that governs our response to being hurt, offended, and mistreated by others. Forgiveness unlocks the prison of resentment that can wither and embitter our hearts.

The finishing touch of the portrait, the virtue that holds all the other ones together in harmony, what St. Paul calls "the bond of perfection," is love. It reminds us of how Jesus himself summarized the commandments:

𝒻 He said to him, "You shall love the Lord your God, with all your heart, with all your soul, and with all your mind. This is the greatest and the first commandment. The second is like it: You shall love your neighbor as yourself. The whole law and the prophets depend on these two commandments.

—Matthew 22:37–40

In the conference, we will examine another aspect of this portrait of a healthy Christian by reviewing the ancient practice of *Lectio Divina*. But for now, let's take some time, in the quiet of our hearts, to prayerfully reflect on what it means to "walk in Christ." The following questions and quotations may help your meditation.

QUESTIONS FOR PERSONAL REFLECTION/GROUP DISCUSSION

1. What does "walking in Christ" mean for me, in my own mind and in my daily life?

2. When I read St. Paul's description of me as "God's holy one, chosen and beloved", how does that make me feel? Why?

3. How consciously and intentionally do I try to "put away" my self-centered tendencies and "put on" Christ-like attitudes and behaviors? In what ways do I feel God encouraging me and helping me in this daily battle?

Put to death, then, the parts of you that are earthly: immorality, impurity, passion, evil desire, and the greed that is idolatry. Because of these the wrath of God is coming [upon the disobedient]. By these you too once conducted yourselves, when you lived in that way. But now you must put them all away: anger, fury, malice, slander, and obscene language out of your mouths. Stop lying to one another, since you have taken off the old self with its practices and have put on the new self, which is being renewed, for knowledge, in the image of its creator.

—Colossians 3:5–10
NABRE

Put on then, as God's chosen ones, holy and beloved, heartfelt compassion, kindness, humility, gentleness, and patience, bearing with one another and forgiving one another, if one has a grievance against another; as the Lord has forgiven you, so must you also do. And over all these put on love, that is, the bond of perfection.

—Colossians 3:12–14
NABRE

And let the peace of Christ control your hearts, the peace into which you were also called in one body. And be thankful. Let the word of Christ dwell in you richly, as in all wisdom you teach and admonish one another, singing psalms, hymns, and spiritual songs with gratitude in your hearts to God. And whatever you do, in word or in deed, do everything in the name of the Lord Jesus, giving thanks to God the Father through him.

—Colossians 3:15–17
NABRE

NOTES

CONFERENCE

*Lectio Divina: Letting the Word of Christ
Dwell in Us Richly*

INTRODUCTION

After warning the Colossians about spiritual worldliness and encouraging them to "walk in Christ," St. Paul changes gears a little bit. When warning about worldly vices, he used the verbs like "put to death" and "put away". When encouraging Christian virtues he used verbs like "put on" and "do". As he continues sketching a portrait of what it means to be "rooted in Christ" and "built upon him", he changes his verbs. He writes:

> And let the peace of Christ control your hearts, the peace into which you were also called in one body. And be thankful. Let the word of Christ dwell in you richly, as in all wisdom you teach and admonish one another, singing psalms, hymns, and spiritual songs with gratitude in your hearts to God.
>
> —Colossians 3:15–16

Notice how in each of those verses St. Paul admonishes us to "let" something happen: "*let* the peace of Christ control your hearts," he writes, and "*let* the word of Christ dwell in you richly".

When people knock on our door, we have the option of keeping them out or letting them in. Keeping them out means doing nothing. It means continuing business as usual in the house. Letting them in means deciding to open the door, giving them permission to enter our personal space. This is what St. Paul is getting at here. We need to give Jesus permission to "control our hearts" with his peace, and to "dwell in us richly" through his word.

In this conference, we will look at a spiritual discipline used by Christians for centuries to open the doors of our hearts and minds to Christ's life-giving peace and redeeming word. It's called *Lectio Divina*, which is Latin for "divine" or "sacred reading."

ANCIENT ORIGINS

The term has a long history. It first appears in written form in St. Benedict's Rule for monks, written in the early sixth century. Rule #48 begins like this:

Idleness is the enemy of the soul. Therefore, the brothers should have specified periods for manual labor as well as for prayerful reading [lectione divina].

In this way, prayerful reading of the Bible and of trustworthy commentaries on the Bible became a regular practice among monks and those who were educated by monks.

At first, this *Lectio Divina* didn't have any particular method. It simply consisted in a slow, prayerful reading of the Sacred Scriptures. It could involve a certain amount of study, but the core of the devotion consisted in a reverential listening in the heart to the inspired Word of God. This form of reading was meant to be a prayer in which the follower of Christ could encounter the person of Christ through the sacred words of the Bible.

In the earliest centuries of Christianity, the Bible was already considered a unique book, a book written by human authors but inspired by the Holy Spirit. The Letter to the Hebrews describes this point of view with a memorable image:

❛Indeed, the word of God is living and effective, sharper than any two-edged sword, penetrating even between soul and spirit, joints and marrow, and able to discern reflections and thoughts of the heart.

—Hebrews 4:12

Reading the Bible prayerfully, therefore, was a way to open the door of one's heart to God's word, one way to "let the word of Christ dwell in you richly."

A RICH HISTORY

The tradition continued through the centuries until a Carthusian monk named Guigo II formalized a particular method of *Lectio Divina* in a book he wrote in the late 1100s. The four steps of this method became the touchstone of *Lectio Divina*, as well as the inspiration for other methods of Christian meditation even up until modern times. With the growth of a more secular and scientific mindset, some modern scholars began questioning the sacred character of the Bible. This challenged the value of prayerful reading of the Scriptures for a time, but with the Second Vatican Council and subsequent Church teaching, *Lectio Divina* has made a comeback.

Pope Benedict XVI, in an address he gave on the fortieth anniversary of the Second Vatican Council's document on divine revelation, actually linked the revival of *Lectio Divina* to a new springtime for the Church. He said:

❛...I would like in particular to recall and recommend the ancient tradition of *Lectio Divina*: the diligent reading of Sacred Scripture accompanied by prayer brings about that intimate dialogue in which the person reading hears God who is speaking, and in praying, responds to him with trusting openness of heart (cf. *Dei Verbum*, n. 25). If it is effectively promoted, this practice will bring to the Church—I am convinced of it—a new spiritual springtime.[2]

In a later address, he described vividly the heart of *Lectio Divina*:

❝Among the many fruits of this biblical springtime I would like to mention the spread of the ancient practice of *Lectio Divina* or "spiritual reading" of Sacred Scripture. It consists in pouring over a biblical text for some time, reading it and rereading it, as it were, "ruminating" on it as the Fathers say and squeezing from it, so to speak, all its "juice", so that it may nourish meditation and contemplation and, like water, succeed in irrigating life itself.[3]

Notice how Pope Benedict doesn't link the revival of *Lectio Divina* only to the monastic life. In fact, he doesn't even mention monks. This is no coincidence.

NOT JUST FOR MONKS

Just a few years later, in 2008, Pope Benedict presided over a Synod of Bishops dedicated to reflecting on the role of the Bible in the life of the Church. In his Post-Synodal Apostolic Exhortation, Pope Benedict XVI once again praised the benefits of *Lectio Divina*, and this time

---

2   Pope Benedict XVI, Address on the Anniversary of *Dei Verbum*, 16 September 2005 (www.vatican.va).

3   Pope Benedict XVI, Angelus, 6 November 2005 (www.vatican.va).

he explicitly pointed out that these benefits are available to every Catholic, to all the faithful. He wrote:

❝The documents produced before and during the Synod mentioned a number of methods for a faith-filled and fruitful approach to sacred Scripture. Yet the greatest attention was paid to *Lectio Divina*, which is truly capable of opening up to the faithful the treasures of God's word, but also of bringing about an encounter with Christ, the living word of God.[4]

So whether you are a monk, a cloistered nun, a clergyman, or a lay person, *Lectio Divina* is a gift for you. It's a gift for all of us, a simple, powerful method for praying the Scriptures, for engaging in Christian meditation, for opening the door and letting the word of Christ dwell in us richly. Let's briefly review the different steps of this method.

LECTIO

Having glimpsed the long history of this practice, we can understand that throughout the centuries a wide variety of *Lectio Divina* styles have emerged. The primary style, however, remains the individual, monastic method first given formal expression by the Carthusian monk, Guigo II. The four steps of his method were actually explained by Pope Benedict in his Exhortation. Let's take a look at each one of them.

The first step is simply to choose a passage from the Bible and read it. The Latin word for "reading" is "lectio." And that's the name of this first step.

---

4   Pope Benedict XVI, Post-Synodal Apostolic Exhortation *Verbum Domini*, 30 September 2010, #87.

Usually, we choose a short passage, similar in length to the passages of Scripture proclaimed during Mass. In fact, the readings from Mass are an excellent choice for *Lectio Divina*.

This *lectio* step isn't like reading a blog or a news headline. The idea here is to read a passage slowly, reverently. You may want to read the passage out loud. You may want to read it two or three times. Let the sacred words resound in your mind, on your lips, and, above all, in your heart.

The reading of the text involves understanding its most basic, literal meaning, understanding, as Pope Benedict XVI puts it, what the biblical text says in itself. Sometimes commentaries or explanatory notes can be helpful in this stage, especially if we are not familiar with the geographical and cultural background of the different books in the Bible.

MEDITATIO

The second step is referred to by the Latin word "meditatio." We translate this as "meditation." The Latin word comes from the verb "meditari" which means to think over, consider, or ponder. In this second step, then, we express our desire to understand what the biblical passage means not just in general terms, but in personal terms. As Pope Benedict puts it, the "meditation" step consists in asking the question: What does the biblical say to us?

Here is where we "let the word of Christ" into our hearts. Here is where we listen to this sacred, living Word of God and allow it to resonate, to challenge, to inspire, to speak to us in a personal way.

Sometimes it helps to ask questions that can aid our reflection: What does this passage tell me about God?

What does it tell me about myself? What does it tell me about how I should act? Some monastic traditions used the questions we associate with journalism long before journalism came into existence: Who is present in this passage? What are they doing? When did it happen and where? Why did events unfold as they did? Questions like these can uncover what God has to say to us personally as we dig deeper into the passage.

Sometimes when we are engaged in this second step, we don't have to do much work at all. Sometime one word or phrase will resound so powerfully in our mind or heart that we know very quickly what message God has for us.

ORATIO

When our pondering of the sacred text has given us some kind of insight, or moved us in some way, we are ready for the third step: *oratio*. This Latin word can be translated in various ways, all of which have the core meaning of speaking forth, of saying something. In this step of *Lectio Divina* we *respond* to what we have heard from God's word with our own words. We ask and answer the question, as Pope Benedict XVI puts it: What do we say to Lord in response to his word?

We may find ourselves moved to ask God for something, either for ourselves or for others. We may find ourselves moved simply to praise God, or to thank him, or to express sorrow for our sins. The important thing in this stage is to truly speak to the Lord from our own hearts, honestly, trusting that he really is listening. In this way, our relationship with God grows.

CONTEMPLATIO

Once we have responded to God's Word with our own words, we are ready for the fourth step, *contemplatio*.

In the first step, we *read* the passage. In the second step, we begin to reflect on its meaning. In the third step, we respond to what has touched our hearts. And in the fourth step, to use Pope Benedict's words, "we take up, as a gift from God, his own way of seeing and judging reality, and ask our selves *what conversion of mind, heart and life is the Lord asking of us?*"[5] The *contemplatio*, then, is a step in which we let the intimate exchange we have experienced in the *meditatio* and *oratio* sink deeply into our souls; we let it *resonate*. We stay with the Lord in a spiritual embrace and enjoy the goodness that we have discovered through prayerfully digging into the Sacred Scriptures.

TWO MONASTIC SECRETS

The monks who initiated this form of Christian prayer lived a different lifestyle than most of us do. So we need to keep two other things in mind if we want to enrich our own spiritual lives with *Lectio Divina*.

First, monastic life creates a habitual atmosphere of recollection and silence. As a result, when a monk sits down to begin a period of prayerful reading of the Bible, he can easily enter into the presence of the Lord and open his heart to hear what God wants to say. Most of us, however, live busy and noisy lives. When we begin a period of *Lectio Divina*, therefore, we usually have to take

---

5   Pope Benedict XVI, *Verbum Domini* #87.

a couple minutes to quiet our souls and turn down the noise, maybe through praying a decade of the Rosary, or writing in a prayer journal, or listening to a beautiful hymn. It can be hard for us to hear God speaking through the Scriptures if we don't do this.

Second, when the end of the *Lectio Divina* period comes for a monk, he knows exactly what the Lord is asking him to do, because his daily life is governed by a strict and specific rule. Most of us, however, have to discern God's will moment by moment. And so, when we finish a period of prayerful reflection on the Scriptures, it is a good idea to take a look forward and ask, still in the context of prayer, how we can apply to our daily life what God has shown us in our prayer. Here's how Pope Benedict describes this intentional conclusion of *Lectio Divina*:

We do well also to remember that the process of *Lectio Divina* is not concluded until it arrives at action (*actio*), which moves the believer to make his or her life a gift for others in charity.[6]

A lot more could be said about this kind of mental prayer, or Christian meditation, but at least now you have been introduced to, or reminded of, this time-tested method for opening the door to God's grace in our lives, for "letting the word of Christ dwell richly" in our hearts and our minds.

Take some time now to reflect prayerfully on the personal questionnaire, which is designed to help you apply these general truths to your particular circumstances.

---

6   Pope Benedict XVI, *Verbum Domini* #87.

PERSONAL QUESTIONNAIRE

1. What is my general attitude towards the Bible? Reverence, indifference, curiosity...

2. How closely do I pay attention to the readings from the Bible proclaimed during every Mass? Do I usually try to hear the one word or phrase that God has to say *to me* while the readings are being proclaimed?

3. How familiar am I with the Bible? Do I feel that I have a solid, basic understanding of its contents and history? If not, what can I do to improve in this area?

4. How often do phrases or passages from the Bible come spontaneously to mind in the course of the ups and downs of my daily life?

5. How do I feel about the idea of spending some time—even just ten or fifteen minutes—in *Lectio Divina* every day? Why do I feel that way? What am I going to do about it?

6. What helps me settle and quiet my mind and heart when I begin a period of personal prayer?

7. How would I explain the four steps of *Lectio Divina* to someone who is hearing about it for the first time: *lectio, meditatio, oratio, contemplatio*?

8. How do I usually finish a period of personal prayer? With a favorite vocal prayer, a prayer of thanksgiving, a resolution to apply what I have meditated on to my daily life…?

9. How often do I ask for advice from trustworthy people about how to grow in my prayer life?

10. When was the last time I read a book about Christian prayer?

NOTES

FURTHER READING

If you feel moved to continue reflecting and praying about this theme, you may find the following books helpful:

Gaudete et Exultate: Apostolic Exhortation on the Call to Holiness in the Modern World
by Pope Francis

Time for God
by Jacques Philippe

A Guide to Christian Meditation
by John Bartunek, LC

The Better Part: A Christ-Centered Resource for Personal Prayer
by John Bartunek, LC

Difficulties in Mental Prayer
by Eugene Boylan, OCR

Praying Scripture for a Change: An Introduction to Lectio Divina
by Tim Gray

EXPLORING MORE

Please visit our website, *RCSpirituality.org,* for more spiritual resources, and follow us on Facebook for regular updates: *facebook.com/RCSpirituality.*

If you would like to support and sponsor a Retreat Guide, please consider making a donation at RCSpirituality.org.

Retreat Guides are a service of Regnum Christi.
RegnumChristi.org

Produced by Coronation Media.
CoronationMedia.com

Developed & Self-published by RCSpirituality.
RCSpirituality.org

Made in United States
Troutdale, OR
08/19/2024

22155769R10037